YOUR KNOWLEDGE HAS VALUE

Lea Lorena Jerns

American Literary History

Klausurvorbereitung

GRIN Verlag

Bibliografische Information der Deutschen Nationalbibliothek:

Die Deutsche Bibliothek verzeichnet diese Publikation in der Deutschen National-
bibliografie; detaillierte bibliografische Daten sind im Internet über http://dnb.d-
nb.de/ abrufbar.

Imprint:

Copyright © 2013 GRIN Verlag GmbH
Druck und Bindung: Books on Demand GmbH, Norderstedt Germany
ISBN: 978-3-656-70666-3

This book at GRIN:

http://www.grin.com/en/e-book/277887/american-literary-history

GRIN - Your knowledge has value

Der GRIN Verlag publiziert seit 1998 wissenschaftliche Arbeiten von Studenten, Hochschullehrern und anderen Akademikern als eBook und gedrucktes Buch. Die Verlagswebsite www.grin.com ist die ideale Plattform zur Veröffentlichung von Hausarbeiten, Abschlussarbeiten, wissenschaftlichen Aufsätzen, Dissertationen und Fachbüchern.

Visit us on the internet:

http://www.grin.com/

http://www.facebook.com/grincom

http://www.twitter.com/grin_com

MODERNISM (ca. 1900-1950)

Historical Background
Three Phases of Literary Modernism
1. Avant-garde (early 20th century) e.g. Dada (go away from old literary traditions)
2. Classic Modernism (after WW I) → high phase= 1920s (& between WWs)
3. late phase (after WW II) (Canonization through new criticism)

Modernism and the Victorians/ Transatlantic Modernism
- many artists move to Europe (esp. Paris) because US wasn't best place for them to live→ living in Europe was cheaper
- too little respect for art in the USA → in Europe greater appreciation of lit.
- very influential period
- expressionism influenced US-American drama and caused it to become high-culture
- WW II not as influential as WW I

High Phase of Literary Modernism – The Jazz Age (1920s)
- Revolt against Victorianism: general disillusionment with civilization after WW I → leads to Primitivism (=particular interest in Afr. Am., Native Am. and other marginalized groups)
- more extensive exchange of cultures characterizes literature and arts
- emphasis on change/make sth. new (= effect of disillusionment as well)
- general increase in living conditions -> middle class can afford cars, vacation…
- automobile industry pioneered mass-production, aviation begins to develop for travelling, advertising becomes important
- "consumer durable revolution" -> people purchased these goods (=lasting longer than one year like cars, TVs or household goods) often on credit → after 1923: new consumer society
- US becomes most influential global player after WW I
- Rise in stock prices during 1920s
- More people live in cities than in countries →literature in urban environment
- Electrical stuff replaced servants of middle class people→ but didn't mean that you lose social status
- Women started to smoke, cut hair short → youth culture
- Alcohol was prohibited→ drinking became fashionable (→ revealed in 1933)
- Radio influential role but more and more film (Hollywood), sports in addition to news on TV
- African Americans had high hopes to improve their living standards/perspectives after WW I → but rather a backlash as blacks were lynched
- Ku-Klux-Clan re-established itself after 35years in underground
- important representative = F. Scott Fitzgerald → innovative writing style (= captures atmospheres; describes cultures, only uses selected items of black culture but white ideal remains; strong color symbolism)

Literary Modernism
- experimentation with narrative technique → representing thoughts, feelings, semi-conscious states through "stream of consciousness" narration, interior monologue, free indirect discourse
- experimentation with literary forms→ often difficult to read→ did this because old forms thought to be limited
- literary texts characterized by fluidity, dynamism, fragmentation, openness
- foregrounding of materiality of language → draw attention to what language can express and show its limits
- literature on urban environment
- prominence of black writers
- "black wing" of literary modernism (Harlem, Jazz Clubs) → starts a bit earlier than white modernism; art had a strict propaganda/political function= "The New Negro" (name for black writers)

Langston Hughes (1902-1967) – high modernism, poems 1920s
- New consciousness of Afr. Am. → going back to history to show that Blacks were part of the emergence of high culturally traditions
- uses black music and black English venecular (=folk) in his poems (thought it had value as cultural issue) → recognizable that jazz and blues structures taken over by him to structure his poems
- most prominent and versatile member of Harlem Renaissance/New Negro Movement (~1900-1930)
  - starts because black movement from south to north after WW I (= great migration)
  - aim= bring about racial and social uplift
  - forms writers used: venecular language, oral story-telling, different poetry forms e.g. sonnet, jazz, blues
- wanted to capture the dominant oral and improvisatory traditions of black culture in written form

- representative of Jazz Poetry
  = uses jazz form, rhythm, content (1. input, 2.statement with other words, 3.
  ironic variation), actually patronized by whites
- chose to focus his works on modern, urban black life
- modelled his stanza forms on the improvisatory rhythms of jazz music
- adapted vocabulary of everyday black speech to poetry
- poems demanded that African Am. be acknowledged as owners of the culture they gave to the U.S. and
  as fully enfranchised Am. citizens
- "The Negro Speaks of Rivers" (1921, 1926)
  o "river" represents: history of humankind, symbol of life, afr. Am. History, cultural memory, soul
  o "my soul has grown deep like rivers": awareness of history and its richness
  o Chronological overview/account of the development of human culture
  o Illustrates identity of black race through time
  o Talking to Afr. Am. community but also to human kind in general, addresses white people
  o Illustrates identity of the black race through time
  o Black race has a heritage like any other race → equal identity as white race

Modern US-American Drama
- Before 1900: theatre as big business (Broadway)→ comedy and melodrama (=exaggerated stereotypical
  contrasts, happy ending after unrealistic turn of story, virtue is rewarded/vice punished, dramatic
  developments to evoke emotion)
- ~1900: still melodrama but more realistic elements
- After 1900: change through European influence→ theatres as high-art (playwrights became central, not
  actors)
- against entertainment orientated commercial theatre, organized around the star system (=actor is center)
- non commercial: Little Theater Movement (small groups, remote locations) → Provincetown Players
- experimentation with stage techniques
- between the two poles expressionism and realism

Eugene O'Neill (1888-1963) modern U.S. Am. Drama (high modernism)
- first major playwright, the first to explore serious themes in the theatre and to experiment with theatrical
  conventions
- mostly associated with US-American drama, even though also other genres and there were also other
  authors influential even before him
- influence of expressionist theatre → central idea= express a subjective view of reality (usually the
  protagonist's), uses sounds and light as major effects, includes psychological dimensions, frequent use
  of symbols
- experiments with techniques to convey inner emotions that usually were not openly expressed in drama
- influence of Greek drama → use of masks, adoption of classical plays
- importance of psychology and psychoanalysis
- critical rereading of US-American history
- tendency for no happy-ending→ reason: chose form of tragedy
- "Emperor Jones" (1920)
  o a station-play (=loose sequence of scenes) 1 act→ classic expressionist form
  o Expressionism: central topics: trauma, social misery, poverty, alienation, Angst → need to find
    new modes of artistic representation/expression → new artistic forms (station-drama/play)
  o tells tale of Brutus Jones, Afr. Am. man, who kills a man, goes to prison, escapes to Caribbean
    Island and sets himself up as emperor
  o his story is recounted in flashbacks as Brutus makes his way through the forest in an attempt to
    escape former "subjects" (the natives) who have rebelled against him
  o ignored standard play divisions of scenes and acts, paid no attention to the expected length of
    plays → quality of intense concentration
  o about a black man→ innovative effect used by white author
  o stage design: "plaster sky dome"=white plaster half igloo which is lit from back → effect: actors
    can appear in color (=realistic) and black and white
  o color symbolism: uniform-> strong colors, golds → looses clothes during
    wood=social decent symbolized, from civilized to primitive ("rebecoming" slave)
  o Smithers= "a dirty white"→ seen from clothes; worst kind of colonizer (has
    alcohol problem, is sneaky, does not learn native language)
    → traditional roles reversed (esp. in opening scene)

- Jones= working and intellect (even though veecular speech)
- Smithers= lazy, cockney accent
- "Tom Toms" = most striking feature, new stage construction → signify Jones' heartbeat →
viewers
  heartbeat might be affected as well → empathy because you want to stop
  them as well; stop when Jones is dead
- o Process of self-understanding and self-exploration
- o Themes: human life itself, conflict of good and evil, racism, imperialism

The Gender of Modernism
- centrality of women as authors, editors and patrons (=wealthy women who supported artists because had few chances to get one of the rare scholarships)
- modernist writing qualities that are associated with femininity: fragmentation, fluidity, discontinuity, irrationality
- importance of subconscious
- new constructions of sexuality → women have sexual desires as well-> becomes more accepted
- importance of consumption, but modernists ambivalent to mass/popular culture
- 1920: suffragette movement successful→ women=full citizens in terms of voting
- Availability of contraceptives→ family size sinks, women can influence number and point of time when children born
- New ways of moving and dressing allowed (bob-haircut, smoking in public, Charleston dance, use of cars, travelling, no more courgettes)
- New household appliances help domestic household a bit
- Visual image/look/body ideals become more important
- "femme fatale"→ Vamp =fashion style
- Very influential movie industry→ first silent movies, after 1920 talkies

Gertrude Stein (1874-1946)
- one of most influential female modern writers
- more radically experimental than most
- pushed language to its limits – and kept on pushing
- work was sometimes literal nonsense but exciting → thought of writing as a craft and language as a medium with its possibilities and limits
- texts hard to read/to access → breaks up hierarchical structures in language = paratactic sentences instead of hypotactic constructions e.g.
- links her writing to Cezanne's painting with dot-method(→ she wants every word to a weight like the single dots) and to democracy (→"the evenness of everybody having a vote")
- language is a medium & not transparent → emphasis on materiality of language
- against logocentrism (=fact that our language has certain structure that we regard as normal)→ wants to disturb these notions through other perspectives and sub-consciousness
- coins term "the lost generation"
- cubist movement= believed that in painting the "representational paintings" conveyed not what people saw but rather what they had learned to think they saw
- friendship with modernist painters important for her → because of them she came to think of words as tangible entities in themselves as well as vehicles conveying meaning or representing reality
- "Tender Buttons" (1916)
  - o poem-like short story → hard to classify (Cubist prose-poem) → closely related to lit. Modernism: both movements wanted to distance themselves from the authoring, one-dimensional view in reality → interpretation of her work: multi-dimensional
  - o collage of domestic objects
  - o more like meditations/free associations with objects, rather than description/def. → emphasis on sounds and rhythm rather than sense of words → ignored/defied connection between words and meanings continually undercutting expectations about order, coherence and associations
  - o departing from conventional meaning, grammar and syntax→ attempts to capture "moments of consciousness" independent from time and memory → writes down what comes to her mind (subconscious forces made visible through writing)
  - o Reduced vocabulary, punctuation, feminist reworking of patriarchal style= uses binary oppositions differently → everything is not less worthy but just different
  - o provides new lexicon of old words

- influenced by movements: present objects from a different/innovative revolutionary perspective (new way of perceiving ordinary objects of daily use which have become so normal that their essence has been forgotten)

Political Advocacy in the 1930s
- economy strongly going down until 1933 → new president Franklin D. Roosevelt
- since then new role of women → achivements esp. of wife Elenore Roosevelt
- US-Am literature in 1930s
  - turn towards more "realistic" narration but not end of modernist experimentation
  - new idea of America: solidarityy, democratic tendencies, working class (≠ only money)
  - documentary impulse→ photography/art produced to document current political situation, e.g. poor woman with children
- Relief programs of US gov't

Zora Neale Hurston (1891-1960)
- Great Depression
- focus on lower middle class, Afr. Am. folk culture
- female self-determination and emergence of a distinct voice→ black venecular used in free indirect discourse
- raising star of Harlem Renaissance (=cultural movement 1920s-30s "New Negro Movement")
- Afr. Am. Narrative→ main interest= achieve black narrative voice , make black dialect (=venecular) function as literary language
- "The Gilded Six-Bits" (1933)
  - short story with omniscient third person narrator
  - use of venecular speech -> deeply emotional, focus on individual
  - "negro"= word for independence and standing up for Afr. Am culture
  - story takes place at Eatonville, Fl = first incorporated all-black town in US
  - several parallels to Hurston's life e.g. Eatonville her hometown until 9, problems with marriage, had to leave school for financial problems
  - marriage/love = main theme of story (->beginning everything is good- trouble husband truly forgives her and continue with rituals from before, but changed situation)
  - sexuality also role (->she betrays husband)
  - money plays important role
  - appearance vs. reality → story shows that Slemmons is not as classy as he pretends
  - protagonists are poor but happy
  - gilded six-bits symbolize fake/being unreal/being white = symbol of fake American Dream
  - rituals symbolize happiness
  - moral of story: do not betray husband and be happy with what you have got!

New Criticism
- 1930: development of first Am. literary canon→ Am. Dream and recognition that Am. literary culture is worth looking at ->Myth and Symbol School (=group of authors who shaped this process of canonization): Puritan view-> US= virgin land (≠ native Am. view: "long invasion"), looks also what influence industrialization has on US
- "New Critics" influential after WW II but esp. 1950s/60s (= group of male white from south) who defined methodology for Am. literary studies→ close reading best thing because they were mostly interested in form of literature ->intrinsic (= point of view, focalization analysis) and extrinsic approach (= relation to context)
- There ideal was William Empson's "Seven Types of Ambiguity" (1930)

Jewish American Literature
- mid 20th century: Am. jewfish finally made it into mainstream → after WW II no more fights against anti-Semitism and because of their skill (which was only then realized and appreciated)

America in the 1950s
- conservative decade, president: Eisenhower, economic boom because after WW II not much destruction in country (benefitted from WW II) →richest & most powerful country in the world

- large number of people joined middle-class, redistribution from bottom to middle → focus on material wealth and social mobility
- new forms of distributing goods= supermarket, new eating habits adapted to TV
- The Beat Generation
    o group of writers centered in SF and NYC in later half of 1950s
    o members shared antagonism towards middle-class values, commercialism and conformity (emphasis on the individual), as well as enthusiasm for the visionary states produced by religious meditation, sexual experience, jazz or drugs → against capitalism
    o expanding one's consciousness through drugs, sex, mystical elements of the Jewish, Christian and Buddhist religion
    o spirituality as an antidote to the mindless materialism of the 1950s
    o 2 meanings of "beat" 1.beaten = outsiders of society
                             2. beatific = felt social, special culture, blissful
    o Writing style: oceanic prose (long sentences that refused establishes sentence formats) in fiction; use if colloquial language, free verse (elaboration on Whitman's free verse (fairly ling lines)

Allen Ginsberg (1926-1997)
- literary genre: epic poem
- leading figure of The Beat Generation (1950s)
- homosexual
- Existentialism: after WW II → philosophy that emphasises individual experiences, responsibilities → Human being in its existence
- "Howl" (1956)
    o experiments with long lines -> wants to imitate natural speech (oceanic prose)
    o free verse (inspiration by Walt Whitman)
    o scenes, characters and situations drawn from Ginsberg's own experience → connected by pronoun "who" in Part 1 as an anaphoric repetition of fixed base, to keep the beat and have a returning point from which one can take off again
      into another direction
    o break with tradition/concepts of what poetry should look like -> also visible in topics
    o topics of Beat Generation also dealt with here, e.g. loneliness, madness, religion, politics, jazz, sexuality (homo & hetero)…
    o dealt with on two stages: 1. personal/private articulation/liberation of self
                                 2. political: liberation of society (gay rights,
                                    freedom of speech)
    o Part 2 "Moloch" → depicts a nightmare image of society (= a society of commercialism, militarism, nationalism, industrialization, sexual suppression…)
    o Part 3 "Rockland"→ written to balance out parts 1&2 and directly addressed to Dadaist Carl Solomon (to whom whole poem is dedicated as well and Ginsberg met at psychiatric institution)
    o Footnote "Holy" → often viewed as Part 4 of poem, counterpart to "Moloch" as similar structures but different perspective
    o Style: individual, open ecstatic expression of thoughts and feelings that were naturally poetic, no meter (free verse)
    o line breaks often determined by breath (G. Explained that all of Howl was an experiment in what could be done with the long line, the longer unit of breath that seemed natural to him
    o Howl combined apocalyptic criticism of the Eisenhower years with celebration of an emerging counterculture

POSTMODERNISM

The 1960s and 70s
- Civil Rights Movement/Black Power → fight for civil equality in general and other movements like: Am. Indian Movement/Red Power, Chicano Movement, Women's liberation Movement, gay and lesbian movement, counterculture (hippies)
  → change in US society and also in literature
- Interrelation of radical political, cultural and social developments →individualization

Postmodernism/New Literary Theory
- Phases of postmodernism
  1. early phase (1960s and 70s)
     → most authors white and male (-> unusual for a movement→ there seems
        to be a white masculinity crisis)
  2. later phase (1970s until today)
     → writing style is taken over by marginalized groups
- Characteristics:
  o experimenting with texts
  o formal innovation
  o foregrounding language
  o Disillusionment
  o interaction with marginalized voices (e.g. non-whites, women…)
     → denial of traditional concepts of structure, subject and language, use of open art forms
     → extreme similarities with modernism
- Features of postmodern texts
  o intertextuality = text draws attention to/quotes earlier texts → foregrounds this borrowing
  o pastiche = putting together a text from other texts -> originality can only emerge from this,
     creates a parodic effect
  o metafiction= text comments on its content itself/on the way they are made

Thomas Pynchon (*1937)
- tries to connect events → complicated and absurd plots
- his sentences often enact the daring freedom he admires in contrast to the institutions of a technological
  society
- "Entropy" (1960)
  - two understandings
  1. thermodynamic = all form and life in universe -> idea that nature tends from
     order to disorder in isolated systems
  2. information theory = all signal, information and written material ever
     produced everywhere
     → always interaction between both understandings in Pynchon's short story
     = top floor: "hothouse" → ??????? temperature inside and outside 37° F
     floor below: party → during four days disorder emerges subtly
  - conclusion: Party = chaos → regularity as "Meatball" uses his energy to get
                             some order
                Hothouse= Regularity → Chaos
  - no real order in story → jumping back and forth all the time

Effects of Feminism and Multiculturalism on US Am. Literature
- linked to different political movements (e.g. Black Power, gays and lesbians…)
- canon= collection of works eb. should supposedly have read, are supposed to be central & of highest
  quality → content = debate
- 3 major ways of how canon was shaped:
  1. new recognition for non-white, female and gay literary voices
  2. reconstruction of literary history
  3. historicization of aesthetic standards
- nowadays more flexible canons/eb. has personal canon
- Black Poetry after 1960s
  → result of civil rights movement that people want to express themselves->many
     chose poetry because one can hold public readings rather than having to
     publish them (= hard & expensive), one can have several short pieces on
     different topics
- Black Women's Literature after 1970
  → wanted to address all facettes and every problem they encounter -> found
     strength within this/their community
  - autobiographic form often uses
  - e.g. Toni Morrison
  - development of black feminist theory

- Slavery in Afr. Am. fiction

Gloria Anzaldúa (1942-2004)
- Background of Chicano Movement:
    o Mexican-American War 1846-1848 → Mexicans (predominantly native Am. and of European descent) became Americans overnight→ "Mexican-Americans"
    o "white" by law, but socially not accepted in that way (e.g. no possibilities to vote, segregated schools =denial of basic human rights)
    o bilingualism not allowed → 1954: "No Spanish Rules"
    o Chicano/Chicana = " the poorest of the poor" originally derogatory meaning but during movement widely used by M-Am,→ for them= positive, self- identifying, try to establish a unique ethnic identity
    o Chicana = specifically identifying Mexican Am. women, particularly in light of their announced aims and the general interest of the Chicano movement
    o 1960s in context of civil rights movement → address negative stereotypes of M-Am. and to end social, educational and employment discrimination as well as racism, exploitation and other political rights including voting rights
- Chicana/o literature suggests that it is interesting to look at Mexican and Am. literature → new type of literature emerges
- Aimed to improve social, economic and political situation of Chicano population
- Helped Mex.Am. to develop new political consciousness and self-determination
- "How to Tame a Wild Tongue" (1987)
    o social commentary of her personal memory
    o autobiographical experience → text's authenticity
    o structured by dividing text and giving parts headlines
    o inclusion of proverbs, sayings and poems, use of imagery → rhythmical text
    o switching to Spanish in a piece mainly written in English (hybridity → also employed in diff. Writing styles: poems, essays, autobiographies)
    o often no translations given = not only did she wish to write in Spanish from time to time, shows reader frustrating feeling Anzaldúa experienced throughout her life, addresses with that parts people who couldn't or wouldn't communicate with her in English → addresses people who could not or didn't want to communicate in English → helps create the narrative richness that characterizes her work
    o poems and sayings underline/support key points of essay = e.g. language is part of culture and it's not good to suppress
    o intention
    o illustrate refusal of rejection of own heritage/identity/language simply for the sake of belonging → be proud of your descent & recognize many dimensions of your culture →show fellow sufferers other people who feel the same → give them hope
    o bring identity problem of Chicanos to society's attention
    o Hybridity = concept that highlights something positive/interesting even though formerly negative biological term
    e.g. Gloria Anzaldùa → focus on borderlands ≠ borderlines → argues that different cultural zones come together and usually one discourse of both is dominant but nevertheless they enter in dialogue → there are problems (she points out those in the beginning) but comes to the conclusion that they are creative and develop new forms as well

Louise Erdrich (*1954)
- daughter of parents with German and French-Indian descent
- member of Indian Tribe in North Dakota
- focuses in her works on Chippewa ->their progression/development in history/across centuries and how they had to arrange with modern habits etc.
- "Fleur" (1977)
    - short story (=chapter 2 Tracks, but first published in magazine)
    - thematizes female savageness and men trying to control it by violence, life in Nat. Am. reservation and indigenous religion/beliefs
    - highly detailed realistic setting invaded by fantastic elements, superstition and myth→ the magical is presented as real

Feminism and US-Am. Literature in the late 20th century
- critique of fictional representations of women
- consciousness-raising via literature to criticize the representations of women by male authors (stereotype: women are either married or die) → revaluation of women's literature
- use of autobiography
- many more texts by women published also by other groups (esp. minorities)
  → reshaping of Am. literary history ->recovering "lost" writers and texts e.g. Charlotte Perkins Gilman "The Yellow Wallpaper"
- Exploration of New Fictional Terrain
  - utopian fiction
  - science fiction
  - crime fiction
- After 1960/70s feminism= diverse
  - Chinese Am. Women's literature→ focus on discrimination of women in society
- Hybridity = concept that highlights something positive/interesting even though formerly negative biological term
  e.g. Gloria Anzaldùa → focus on borderlands ≠ borderlines -> argues that different cultural zones come together and usually one discourse of both is dominant but nevertheless they enter in dialogue → there are problems (she points out those in the beginning) but comes to the conclusion that they are creative and develop new forms as well
- L=A=N=G=U=A=G=E poetry
  → special wing of poetry experimenting with written language which views language as a sign system, rather than focussing on oral traditions
- Black Gay Poets
  → also grouping during that time but focussing on oral traditions in poems

Development of Literary Theory
- from 1960s onwards theory changes (-> away from new criticism with its main means close reading), it is claimed that:
  - language shapes our understanding of reality
  - language = arbitrary system (= not transparent) -> it is conevtional
  - language precedes subjectivity (= one is born into existing language system to use rather than developing one by your own
- important theorists: Michel Foucault, Jacques Derrida

Toni Morrison (*1931)
- Afr. Am. Pulitzer Prize ("Beloved") and Literature Nobel Prize winner (1993, 1st Afr. Am. women)
- Primarily novelist of great importance in her own right and has been the central figure in putting fiction by and about Afr.Am. women at the forefront of the late 20th century literary canon
- "Recitatif" (1983/1989)
  o the only short story by Morrison
  o themes: two girls of incompetent mothers are dumped in a shelter for children, moral guilt and putative memorization of past incidents, racial codes: color, class, family, religion, culture, friendship across race boundaries (→ emotional side is shared)
  o nowhere explicitly stated who of two girls is black and white → hints: R. screaming at T. for kicking a black woman (=awareness of racial difference), R. married to IBM-guy ->upper class, R. Illiterate → everything still uncertain! Maybe allusion to famous people: T. Tharp = white, Roberta Plack= white
  o major topic = race → racial ambiguity created→ forces us to see stereotypes we have internalized = M. plays with racial codes → we are made to think that not everybody fits into stereotypes = M. (tries to) deconstruct concept of race
  o refuses to identify her characters by race, although
  o it's about how people are racial categories and how we form groups
  o "Recitatif"= French → musical term referring to a segment in an opera sung in a way that resembles speech -> generally a solo that helps plot to progress, a rendition of memorized information

Tony Kushner (*1956)
- New Yorker of Jewish intellectual family, liberal, homosexual

- during youth experiences mild anti-Semitism and strong homophobia
- context:
    o US under Reagan administration (1981-89) and early years of AIDS epidemic
    o 70s: US tremendous pessimism based on damage done by Vietnam War, race riots, oil crisis and international terrorism → Reagan's project = restore pride and optimism -> emphasizing issues of morality, religion and traditional family values and partly campaigned against sexual liberation of gay community → extremely conservative political climate
    o Reference to McCarthyism: against communists and homosexuals
- "Angels in America" (1995)
    o epic poem (= plot unfolds over many settings and time span, involves many characters and more than one story line) consisting of two parts ("Millennium Approaches" and "Perestroika") making up entire plot
    o no main character → collective approach of 8 characters, focus on 2 couples (→ 1 gay, 1 married), other characters by the majority gay + Jewish/Republican/Mormon → cannot say: THE gay → but diverse
    o heavily influenced by Brecht's political theatre and notion of epic theatre
    o rapid scene changes; switching between real and imagined, natural and supernatural, past and present
    o not merely realistic: angels appear (symbolic connotations: messenger mediate between diff. worlds)
    o making use of "split scenes" (=two scenes take place at same time on one stage (cf. TV) → show parallels → considered to be ultimately innovative to Am. theatre
    o not strictly speaking realistic as it has real angels (->presented the way angels "are") → f(x)= mediate between two worlds
    o central issue: what does it mean to be gay?! → Look at issue from different perspectives → can one classify gay? Does homosexuality define your identity? → characters: all gay but of diff. pol. views, religious groups, ethnicities
    o text links q. of AIDS with what it means to be homosexual: government no interest in research of AIDS → AIDS as punishment for being gay
    o further topic that formerly was taboo: sexual harassment

Neo-Realism
- 1990s new literary movement → change away from post-modernist towards something reminiscing of realism (-> forerunner of movement was "New Journalism" which was influenced by marginalized literature
- Fuzzy term because postmodern and realist elements overlap
- Main representative: Paul Auster
- Many (American) people say: 9/11 = end of post-modernism as it has shown that not everything is fiction but reality is true and has consequences for everybody

South-Asian American writers
- since change immigration law in 1965 influx from India, Bangladesh, Pakistan and Sri Lanka -> good education, often also capital
- movement does not stop (=they don't stay at US, but spend some month here, some back home) → hybrid

Jhumpa Lahiri (*1967)
- daughter of Indian immigrant parents born in London, age of 3: moved to USA
- diasporic writer → related themes but also "normal" themes e.g. family life, generation conflict
- "Hell-Heaven" (2004)
    o wants to stress: in a diaspora one has to change and adopt other topics: displacement, assimilation, alienation, stereotypes, generation conflicts, prejudice, hybridity, identity, cultural heritage, family
    o use of focalization: daughter reflects on her childhood and her mother's life in retrospective → going back and forth in between sometimes comments like "Now I know that…" → daughter chosen because she is the one within conflict: dichotomy being American and/or (?) Indian
    o multi-perspectivity in text
    o question of gender construction and class

- fictive kinship (biological relation to people) → immigrants form new social relations + establish new sorts of social relations based on existing family models
- importance of food

Jonathan Safran Foer (*1977)

- Jewish-American writer
- Visual writing = non-traditional writing technique, with visual part of writing itself → tools not decorative or extraneous but a key to the writing itself
- First impression of 9/11 was visual (TV) → images of towers collapsing dominated peoples impression
- "Extremely Loud and Incredibly Close" (2005)
  - response to 9/11 → US/global trauma addressed through eyes of 9year old Oskar (= main narrator -> Grandparents are "sub-narrators") and shows its effect on this family's everyday life
  - father was on the upper floors of the World Trade Center when the jets crashed into the Twin Towers
  - to fight his grief and quell his imagination, Oskar embarks on a quest to find what he hopes is his father's most illuminating secret
  - In service of this quest, Oskar conquers many of his irrational fears and comforts other damaged souls
  - main themes: death, loss, emotional trauma → many people in story dealing (differently) with these problems
  - manual of letting go: Oscar has to learn that
  - visual writing in the novel
  - e.g.: some pages= blank, page with one sentence each, text overlapping each other, three pages of numbers, pictures
  - images used to connect ideas, themes, emotions and perspectives alluded to on earlier page
  - last 15 pages: flip-book collection of pictures of the falling man in reverse order→ seems falling upwards the World Trade Center → pictures reflect Oskar's mind but don't really add anything to the novel